Once upon a time, Taylor the Toot
alone on the farm. Until one day, I
home two new turkeys. Their name
Max and this is their story...

Taylor the Tooting Turkey and the Tooting Wars

By Humor Heals Us

When Farmer Tom left, Max was ready to retaliate.

He released deadly tank toots.

Before you knew it, Austin and Taylor had been blasted.

Once they recovered, Austin had only one thing in mind.

He had held his toot in all day until the perfect moment. The time had come.

The tooting wars went on all day.
Which turkey won? You decide.

Austin wasn't going to be outdone. So he let out a **toot torpedo.** It sounded like the farm was going to explode.

Taylor fought back with a **topspin toot** that kept spinning its awful smell in circular motions.

And Max decided on some **tomahawk toots**.

Then, it was Austin's turn again. Just as he was releasing one, his toot collided with the other two turkey toots. And it created a **toot tsunami**. The collision was so big, they were almost all obliterated.

The turkeys agreed to end the tooting wars before they all turned to dust.

To celebrate the end of the toot wars, a toot selfie was in order. They all tooted and then smiled for the camera!

Hope I stink so much he doesn't pick me for the BIG DAY.

Made in the USA
Las Vegas, NV
09 November 2024

11441700R00021